Best Editorial Cartoons of 1972

BEST EDITORIAL CARTOONS OF 1972

A Pictorial History of the Year

Edited by
CHARLES BROOKS

Foreword by Scott Long

PENSACOLA JUNIOR COLLEGE
MILTON CENTER LIBRARY

PELICAN PUBLISHING COMPANY

GRETNA 1973

Copyright © 1973
Charles G. Brooks
All rights reserved
ISBN: 911116-95-8
First printing

Acknowledgments are made to the following for special permission to use copyrighted material in this volume.

Editorial cartoons by Jeff MacNelly, © Chicago Tribune—New York News Syndicate; by Brickman, © Washington Star Syndicate and King Features; by Tom Darcy, © Los Angeles Times Syndicate; by Jim Ivey, © Ben Roth Agency; by Ranan Lurie, © United Feature Syndicate; by Frank Interlandi, © Los Angeles Times Syndicate; by Dick Wallmeyer, © Register and Tribune Syndicate; by Dennis Renault, © McClatchey Newspapers of California; by Al Wetzel, © Ben Roth Agency; by Jim Berry, © NEA; by Hugh Haynie, © Los Angeles Times Syndicate; by L. D. Warren, © McNaught Syndicate; by Gar Schmitt, © Gar Schmitt Syndicate; by Pat Oliphant, © Los Angeles Times Syndicate; by Ben Wicks, © Toronto Sun Syndicate; by Milt Morris, © Associated Press; by Bill Crawford, © NEA; by Lou Grant, © Los Angeles Times Syndicate; by Jack Bender, © Ben Roth Agency; by Bill Graham, © Ben Roth Agency; by Dan Dowling, © Publishers—Hall Syndicate.

In the event any necessary permissions for the use of copyrighted material have been omitted through error, acknowledgments and apologies will be made.

Manufactured in the United States of America
by Benson Printing Company, Nashville, Tennessee

Published by Pelican Publishing Company, Inc.
630 Burmaster Street, Gretna, Louisiana 70053
Book and jacket design by J. Barney McKee

74-5834 MCL

Dedicated to politicians everywhere, of all parties and persuasions, whose words and acts daily impel the editorial cartoonist's pen.

Contents

Foreword

Editorial cartoons are contemporary stuff, the products of a living, sometimes livid, moment. They are intended for the here and now, reflecting graphic opinions about controversial events that are still breathing heavily. They offer brash and momentary judgments about living persons freshly bruised. They represent lively art and living human history. And if they find themselves enshrined in books as mementoes of fierce or comic encounters, as reminders of historic moments that have long since passed away, it is only by happenstance. For we cartoonists do not draw for the ages. We draw for today.

Yesterday is past, and tomorrow, perhaps, we editorial cartoonists may live on in the happy hunting grounds of historians. But today we stand beside the stove in the heat of the kitchen, exposed and dripping wet, stirring various and simmering political pots in our several ways. We are preparing and drawing our own opinions. We cannot be objective enough to draw conscious history, for we cannot remain outside the political arena.

Never mind that some of us seem to be sniggling in the bleachers or sulking on the sidelines while others are actively groaning on the playing field! Political cartoonists, like politicians, are all caught up in the deadly serious sport of self-government. Each approaches the game differently, with varying talents, but both are engaged in the same enterprise. We are trying to make democracy work.

Cartoonists comprise but a small part of a free press. In America, the press is free by design and enjoys a special, protected status. The press has an obligation to inform, to tell the citizenry the truth about itself and the truth about the actions of its governors, and must therefore be insulated from angry reprisal. To find these truths, the press must also remain skeptical of, and aloof from, those who govern. The press is, in reality, an unofficial arm of government. It is not elected. It is competitive, self-appointed and self-supported. It must be both protected and responsible because it is essential to the success of democracy.

This is the social framework, the political climate, within which we cartoonists work today—living, as it were, by our wits and wisdom and by a few congenital gifts. Just as the climate of the world is ever-changing, so society must change. But as our French colleague Daumier wrote a century ago, "One must be of one's times."

Times do change. Cartoons, for example, were not always drawn on paper. Our art is ancient—older than government, older than the press, paper, papyrus or the written word, older than even civilization itself. Surely, cartooning finds its origins in the fears and superstitions of primitives. And surely, the first exaggerated figures were painted or chiseled on the walls of prehistoric caves or sketched by a finger in flat sand or carved from stone or bone or wood or fashioned out of clay and out of human apprehension, all in an effort to placate gods or con evil spirits or lay a curse upon the enemies of early man. The art of caricature or cartooning must be as old as the human hand.

For what is caricature? The word, derived from both French and Italian, means "to exaggerate, to distort, to ridicule, to burlesque . . . "; in other words, to attack something, a person, an idea or manners by distortion and ridicule. A cartoon is simply pictorial satire, aimed at people and society and using exaggeration, however blunt or subtle, to register a telling criticism. Frequently it is political.

In the English-speaking world, we are known as cartoonists. Elsewhere, we usually are referred to as caricaturists. It makes no difference. Our art has flourished in the past, beginning in sixteenth century Italy, then spreading to France and Britain, to all of Europe and eventually to all the world, and it still flourishes in modern times. Crude, bumptious, effective cartoons abounded in America from the tumultuous times before the Revolution up to the Civil War. Then, beginning with the Civil War and the creative genius of Thomas Nast, cartooning in America developed a sophistication as an art that knows no superiors anywhere, only peers.

A political cartoon can be an awesome weapon, even poisonous, some would say. It can floor an argument with a single, devastating blow. Although only an imaginary picture, a cartoon can reach beyond words and reason and set a torch to emotions. Our primeval impulses and unsuspected prejudices, our grandest yearnings and basest instincts, our greed, our greatness, our loves and hates are all stuffed into subconscious closets of our humanness, tangled and unclassified and more than half-forgotten. In the instant of an image, they can all come tumbling out to form a ready tinder.

A cartoon can break the language barrier and convey a common meaning to all men everywhere. It can anger us, it can make us laugh, it can make us weep. It thrives on crisis and must be used with caution.

Rightly, then, one may question why we would use such a weapon at all. Why distort and malign? Why ridicule? Why exaggerate? If one must draw pictures, why not stick to the facts? Why not tell it as it is? Why, indeed? Because a cartoon is a most effective way of telling the truth. A cartoonist attempts to tell it as it *really* is, the real truth as he sees it. As cartoonists we will admit that we are liars. We will admit that what we draw in our cartoons never really happens in the way we depict it. Almost everything we draw is graphic, artistic fabrication—a lie!

Let me offer one example. Some time ago, after three political assassinations had stunned the nation, I drew a cartoon entitled "The Great Seal of the Presidency." It showed a speakers' platform and a lectern, complete with microphones and an American flag. On the front of the lectern, where the Presidential Seal normally would be mounted, I drew a huge target, a bullseye. Obviously, this was not the literal, objective truth. The scene did not happen, nor does it exist today. I have never seen such a lectern. I invented it, and therefore it is a lie. Why, then, did I draw it?

FOREWORD

I did so because it seemed to me to represent the truth—or, rather, several truths. Able, ambitious men will always seek the Presidency. It is their goal, their target. All of us have thrown verbal rocks at one President or another. Some have attempted to kill the man, and several have succeeded. "The Great Seal of the Presidency" was a sad drawing, but so true!

This, then, is our journalistic permit, our artistic license to exaggerate and distort in order to convey what we believe to be true at a given moment. This is hardly objective reporting. To the contrary, it is entirely subjective and personal. Thus, our cartoons bear our signatures. They reflect only our own opinions, and we reserve the right to change our minds tomorrow.

Indeed, we may exaggerate anything in our cartoons—a man's features, his stature, his idiosyncracies—if it will strengthen what we want to say about the subject. We may use old symbols, such as an elephant or a donkey, to enhance comprehension, or we may invent new symbols to represent abstract notions, such as the Cold War or the Gross National Product. We may animate a tree, a rock, an auto or the earth itself; we could even turn the late General DeGaulle into a living alp! Everything is fair game for our imaginations if it will help make a point and speed our reader's grasp of what we intend to say. At best we have but two seconds of our reader's attention. If we have not attracted him within that time, his mind will wander elsewhere.

In an imperfect world, of course, our freedom is not totally free. The luckiest of us cartoon within the confines of an honest understanding: we are not required to draw anything that violates our own beliefs; conversely, our editors are not obliged to print everything we draw. All cartoonists no doubt prize certain drawings that have never seen a newsstand, but even the best of us work, as we must be free to work, with a minimum of inhibition.

Editorial cartoonists are a species small in number. There are, perhaps, 130 to 140 of us drawing in North America today. We represent all ages and political hues, and we often disagree. But we sight down the barrel of the same gun: our art. We are a minority within a minority within a minority, and we often are a minority of one.

The working press comprises only a fraction of the people on our continent, and most members of the press try to tell what is happening in the world with the greatest objectivity their human frailty can muster. A few of us, however, only a handful, attempt to analyze what is happening and offer opinions about men and events—a hazardous task, indeed. While editorial writers may remain anonymous, political columnists and political cartoonists sign their opinions and thus become highly visible and vulnerable. Ours is a lonely profession. Usually, there is only one cartoonist at any given station. Sometimes, when we are obliged to defend our work and our working eccentricities, we can seem to be, and perhaps are, prima donnas . . . even to our brethren in the business.

But here we are—110 of us—brought together in the pages of a book. In

FOREWORD

this volume, we hope we leaven the whole loaf. We hope to offer the reader a flicker of insight, an instant of mirth, perhaps a guffaw, and even a measure of courageous dissent!

If some cartoon herein should mindlessly offend, we apologize. No offense should be *un*intentional. But if a cartoon purposely offends, please forgive us. It is merely a part of our function in the scheme of modern things. We are of our times.

Scott Long
Minneapolis Tribune

Preface

This volume, the first in a projected annual series, provides a pictorial history of the major news events of 1972, as reflected in the work of the nation's leading editorial cartoonists.

In addition to the primary historical purpose, this book hopefully will achieve two notable objectives: the further advancement of the Association of American Editorial Cartoonists and its professional standing as an integral part of American news reporting and comment; and a wider circulation of the highly varied ideas and efforts of these craftsmen.

The editorial cartoons contained in this volume were selected from the many hundreds produced during 1972 by 110 editorial cartoonists in the United States and Canada. Choosing the best from such a vast number was a formidable task, indeed. Best is always relative and choice necessarily subjective. It should be noted that in the selection process some deserving editorial cartoons no doubt escaped attention; others, perhaps of equal merit, were omitted because of requirements of subject and space.

I appreciate the cooperation of the editorial cartoonists represented here who took time from their busy schedules to review their work and submit their choices of their best efforts of the year. A special word of appreciation also is due the media these cartoonists represent—newspapers, magazines, television stations and syndicates—for permission to reprint the works contained in this unique collection of pictorial excellence.

Award-Winning Cartoons

1972 PULITZER PRIZE

JEFFREY K. MACNELLY

Editorial Cartoonist
Richmond News Leader

Born September 17, 1947 in New York City; son of C. L. MacNelly, portrait painter and former publisher of the *Saturday Evening Post*; attended the University of North Carolina; National Newspaper Association Award for best weekly newspaper editorial cartoon, 1970; cartoonist, *Chapel Hill Weekly*, 1968–70; editorial cartoonist, *Richmond News Leader*, since 1970; cartoons syndicated by the Chicago Tribune—New York News Syndicate.

1971 SIGMA DELTA CHI AWARD
(Selected in 1972)

"Oh, yes, sir. They're very nice
Moon rocks, thank you, sir"

HUGH S. HAYNIE

Editorial Cartoonist
Louisville Courier-Journal

Born February 6, 1927 in Reedville, Virginia; A.B., William and Mary College, 1950; L.H.D., University of Louisville, 1968; Phi Beta Kappa; Omicron Delta Kappa; named one of Ten Outstanding Young Men of the Nation by the U.S. Junior Chamber of Commerce, 1962; National Headliners Club Award, 1966; Freedoms Foundation Medal, 1966, 1970; cartoonist, *Richmond Times-Dispatch*, 1950-53, *Greensboro Daily News*, 1953-55 and 1956-58, and *Atlanta Journal*, 1955-56; editorial cartoonist, *Louisville Courier-Journal*, since 1958; cartoons syndicated by the Los Angeles Times Syndicate.

1972 NATIONAL HEADLINERS CLUB AWARD

JACOB BURCK

Editorial Cartoonist
Chicago Sun-Times

Born January 10, 1907; attended Cleveland School of Art, New York Art Students League; portrait painter, muralist; illustrator, *St. Louis Post-Dispatch*, 1937; editorial cartoonist, *Chicago Times*, and its successor, *Chicago Sun-Times*, since 1938; Pulitzer Prize, 1941; Sigma Delta Chi Award, 1942; Birmingham (Ala.) Museum of Art Award for editorial cartooning, 1958.

Best Editorial Cartoons of 1972

Campaign Politics

Campaign politics dominated the news in 1972 and provided editorial cartoonists everywhere with a rare field day.

While President Richard Nixon was rolling up one of the largest victory margins in history over Democratic challenger George McGovern, Republican Congressional candidates fared less well, and the Democrats retained control of both houses of Congress.

Throughout the campaign, McGovern groped for an issue that would revitalize his campaign, but none was forthcoming. Labeled anti-defense and pro-amnesty, downgraded by the polls and saddled with running mate problems, McGovern found usually loyal Democrats deserting the party in record numbers. Nixon won 61 percent of the vote and carried 49 states, losing only Massachusetts and the District of Columbia.

KARL HUBENTHAL
Courtesy Los Angeles
Herald-Examiner

'We've Now Reached Our Campaign Turning Point'

DON HESSE
Courtesy St. Louis Globe-Democrat

'And to think, I once was a 97-pound weakling'

CARL LARSEN
Courtesy Richmond Times-Dispatch

'HAVE YOU TRIED THE PILL?'

L. D. WARREN
Cincinnati Enquirer
© McNaught Syndicate

'WHAT HAPPENED TO OUR MAINSTREAM?'

DICK WALLMEYER
Long Beach Press-Telegram
© Register and Tribune Syndicate

INDEPENDENT, PRESS-TELEGRAM

MacNELLY THE RICHMOND NEWS LEADER ©1972 CHICAGO TRIBUNE.

'HIGHER.'

FF MACNELLY
chmond News Leader
Chicago Tribune—New York
News Syndicate

ED VALTMAN
Courtesy Hartford Times

'Welcome aboard, Sarge! I know you've sailed a lot with the Kennedys. You're just the man I need'

L. D. WARREN
Cincinnati Enquirer
© McNaught Syndicate

5

WAYNE STAYSKAL
Courtesy Chicago Today

the small society   by Brickman

Washington Star Syndicate, Inc.

BRICKMAN
© Washington Star Syndicate and
King Features

'Know Anybody That Wants To Be My Copilot?'

CHARLES WERNER
Courtesy Indianapolis Star

JEFF YOHN
Courtesy Sacramento Union

As *Hy Rosen* Sees It

"YOU GUYS GOT US IN ... NOW GET US OUT!"

HY ROSEN
Courtesy Albany Times-Union

Acute Case of McGovernitus

ROBERT ZSCHIESCHE
Courtesy Greensboro Daily News

7

AL WETZEL
American Opinion
© Ben Roth Agency

"Why don't people believe me when I claim to be a disciple of General Eisenhower?"

MOST HAPPY FELLA

BRUCE SHANKS
Courtesy Buffalo Evening News

© 1972, Buffalo Evening News, Inc.

'You Don't Mind If I Use Your Name Now and Then?'

JOHN STAMPONE
Courtesy Army Times

'That's Where Tom Dewey Went Off Th'...Say, Aren't We Going Kind Of Fast?'

CHARLES WERNER
Courtesy Indianapolis Star

IT'S BEGINNING TO SHOW, SPIRO

BRUCE SHANKS
Courtesy Buffalo Evening News

DAVID SIMPSON
Courtesy Tulsa Tribune

9

JOHN STAMPONE
Courtesy Army Times

BILL SANDERS
Courtesy Milwaukee Journal

THE MILWAUKEE JOURNAL

the small society   by Brickman

BRICKMAN
© Washington Star Syndicate and
King Features

PAT OLIPHANT
Denver Post
© Los Angeles Times Syndicate

Practically No Coattails At All

ELDON PLETCHER
*Courtesy New Orleans
Times-Picayune*

DENNIS RENAULT
© McClatchey Newspapers
of California

'This Must Be Like Acupuncture; I Don't Feel A Thing.'

FRANKLIN MORSE
Courtesy Hearst Publications

HEAD OF THE PARTY

THE VICTOR

REG MANNING
Courtesy Arizona Republic

PAT OLIPHANT
Denver Post
© Los Angeles Times Syndicate

SARDINES

SCOTT LONG
Courtesy Minneapolis Tribune

"EDMUND? ARE YOU ALL RIGHT?"

FRANKLIN MORSE
Courtesy Hearst Publication.

"Don't Jump, Larry!"

HAROLD MAPLES
Courtesy Fort Worth Star-Telegram

'Well, it's a start. You've shot your horse'

GUERNSEY LEPELLEY
Courtesy Christian Science Monitor

JIM IVEY
Orlando Sentinel
© Ben Roth Agency

MINNEAPOLIS STAR
ROY JUSTUS
Courtesy Minneapolis Star

BELOW OLYMPUS   By Interlandi

FRANK INTERLANDI
© Los Angeles Times Syndicate

"Oh, it feels so-o-o-o good!"

JON KENNEDY
Courtesy Arkansas Democr

'Not so fast, Ted'

14

'What, Me Worry?'

CARL LARSEN
Courtesy Richmond Times-Dispatch

Still Trying to Pull a Rabbit Out of the Hat

ED HOLLAND
Courtesy Chicago Tribune

KARL HUBENTHAL
*Courtesy Los Angeles
Herald-Examiner*

ROBERT GRAYSMITH
Courtesy San Francisco Chronicle

"I'm going to be on the ticket, Mr. President? What a surprise . . . I never suspected . . ."

"It's From the President. He Says at First He Was Against The 20% Increase and Only for a 5% Increase But Now He's for a 20% Increase Since It's So Close To Election Time and It's Signed, 'Tricky Dicky'."

BILL GRAHAM
Arkansas Gazette
© Ben Roth Agency

NEW IMAGE

EDDIE GERMANO
Courtesy Brockton Daily Enterprise

WHY NOT?

CRITICISM OF DECEPTIVE ADVERTISING

CANDIDATES PROMISING INSTANT SOLUTIONS TO COMPLEX PROBLEMS

CONSUMER ADVOCATES

LOUIS GOODWIN
Courtesy Columbus (O.) Dispatch

ART HENRIKSON
Courtesy Des Plaines (Ill.) Herald

OVER SPENDING

BUDGET

ADMINISTRATION

CONGRESS

ELECTION YEAR GOOD WILL

Getting carried away

ED FISCHER
Courtesy Omaha World-Herald

CY HUNGERFORD
Courtesy Pittsburgh Post-Gazette

ENGELHARDT
TOM ENGELHARDT
Courtesy St. Louis Post-Dispatch

The 1984 Election Is Coming A Little Early

JACK JURDEN
Courtesy Wilmington Evening
Journal-News

'John.' 'Martha.' 'John!' 'Martha!'

GOOD SENSE

WALTER KRAWIEC
Courtesy Chicago Polish Daily News

DEMOCRATIC
PRESIDENTIAL
NOMINEE
FOR '72

LEW HARSH
Courtesy Scranton Times

The Pieces are Falling into Place

" I CANNOT TELL A LIE ... I'M A DEMOCRAT "

BOB TAYLOR
Courtesy Dallas Times Herald

JERRY DOYLE
Courtesy Philadelphia Daily News

A Hard Pose To Hold

'NIXON IS THE PEACE CANDIDATE'–POLLS

ENGELHARDT
TOM ENGLEHARDT
Courtesy St. Louis Post-Dispatch

'Coo-o-o'

DAN DOWLING
Kansas City Star
© Publishers-Hall Syndicate

" IT USUALLY HAS LOTS OF PEPPER AND IS SERVED PIPING HOT! "

ED FISCHER
Courtesy Omaha World-Herald

'Watch It. He's the Guy Who Hasn't Paid for '68 Yet'

'First—We'll Give You a Shot of Anesthetic'

DON HESSE
Courtesy St. Louis Globe-Democrat

"TO KEEP FROM OFFENDING THE McGOVERN PEOPLE, I PROMISE NOT TO BACK UP!"

CHARLES BROOKS
Courtesy Birmingham (Ala.) News

'THE PROBLEM'S NOT IN YOUR SET!'

GIB CROCKETT
Courtesy Washington Star

'I'd Like to Read You One About a Tortoise and a Hare'

PAP DEAN
Courtesy Shreveport Times

ABRAHAM WHO ?

MERLE CUNNINGTON
Courtesy Valley News (Calif.)

HUGH HAYNIE
Louisville Courier-Journal
© Los Angeles Times Syndicate

JACK BENDER
Waterloo Courier
© Ben Roth Agency

DOUG MARLETTE
Courtesy Charlotte Observer

MARLETTE
THE CHARLOTTE OBSERVER

"STRANGE—I THOUGHT WHEN WE GO UP, HE GOES DOWN!"

DRAPER HILL
*Courtesy Memphis
Commercial Appeal*

DICK WALLMEYER
Long Beach Press-Telegram
Ⓒ Register and Tribune Syndicate

The Spiro of '76

AUTH
THE PHILADELPHIA INQUIRER

TONY AUTH
Courtesy Philadelphia Inquirer

'I'M SURE WE CAN PUT IT ALL TOGETHER, FRANK!'

GIB CROCKETT
Courtesy Washington Star

ED ASHLEY
Courtesy Toledo Blade

'I'm sorry, Martha! But in a campaign
every word uttered can make a difference!'

ED VALTMAN
Courtesy Hartford Times

KEN ALEXANDER
Courtesy San Francisco Examiner

'I'll hang up my guns, if you'll hang up your phone'

JON KENNEDY
Courtesy Arkansas Democrat

The Bad News Must Be Bad

"BETTER GET OUT O' THIS FELLA'S PATH- TH' WAY HE'S SWINGIN', ANYBODY'S LIABLE TO GET HIT."

THE SHREVEPORT TIMES 9-26-72

PAP DEAN
Courtesy Shreveport Times

"Senator Muskie Says He Will Continue the Race"

GENE BASSETT
Courtesy Scripps-Howard Newspapers

JOHN CHASE
Courtesy WDSU-TV, New Orleans

"NOW THAT'S WHAT I CALL CONFIDENCE... THE GAME DOESN'T START TILL NOVEMBER 7"

GENE BASSETT
Courtesy Scripps-Howard Newspapers

"YOU BLASTED IDIOT! I KEEP TELLING YOU I'M FEELING FINE!"

CHARLES BROOKS
Courtesy Birmingham (Ala.) News

CHARLES BISSELL
Courtesy Nashville Tennessean

'Sorry, Boss, Vacation's About Over'

Political Science

DENNIS RENAULT
© McClatchey Newspapers
of California

BOB MURPHY
Courtesy Manchester Union-Leader

"Who is George McGovern and why is he saying those terrible things about me?"

DRAPER HILL
*Courtesy Memphis
Commercial Appeal*

JACK BENDER
Waterloo Courier
© Ben Roth Agency

MILT MORRIS
© Associated Press

RALPH VINSON
Courtesy New Orleans States-Item

AFTER THE BALL IS OVER . . .

JOHN CHASE
Courtesy WDSU-TV, New Orleans

74-5834 MCL

"I KNEW IT WAS GOING TO BE UPHILL, BUT___"

LOU GRANT
Oakland Tribune
© Los Angeles Times Syndicate

"Thou mayest announce to the assembled multitudes that my governmental reorganization is complete."

HUGH HAYNIE
Louisville Courier-Journal
© Los Angeles Times Syndicate

The Eagleton Affair

Sen. Thomas Eagleton of Missouri, nominated as the Vice Presidential running mate of George McGovern, was dropped from the ticket after disclosures of his having undergone psychiatric treatment on several occasions. The action came after McGovern had announced: "I'm 1,000 percent behind Eagleton." The action further divided the Democratic Party and no doubt ensured McGovern's defeat. It was widely rumored that at least half a dozen prominent Democrats declined to accept the vacated candidacy before it was filled by Sargent Shriver.

Baldy

BALDY
Courtesy Atlanta Constitution

"...NOW, SENATOR EAGLETON, LET'S BURY THE HATCHET!"

Devalued

REG MANNING
Courtesy Arizona Republic

JACK JURDEN
*Courtesy Wilmington Evening
Journal-News*

*'–And If Anyone Around Here So Much As Hints
He Should Have His Head Examined, He's Fired!'*

CHARLES WERNER
Courtesy Indianapolis Star

TONY AUTH
Courtesy Philadelphia Inquirer

PUTTING IT ALL TOGETHER

BOB HOWIE
Courtesy Jackson (Miss.) Daily News

BLAINE
Courtesy The Spectator, Canada

TOM CURTIS
Courtesy Milwaukee Sentinel

"Congratulations, Mr. Shriver!"

BILL McCLANAHAN
Courtesy Dallas Morning News

Another Battle Scar

FRIENDLY PERSUASION

BOB PALMER
SPRINGFIELD LEADER-PRESS

8-1-72

BOB PALMER
Courtesy Springfield (Mo.)
Leader-Press

ROBERT GRAYSMITH
Courtesy San Francisco Chronicle

"Better you than the party, Tom"

McGovern's Albatross

ROBERT ZSCHIESCHE
Courtesy Greensboro Daily News

KEN DOLAN
Courtesy Flint Journal

Vietnam

After more than a decade of fighting, approximately 46,000 American combat deaths and the expenditure of nearly $130 billion, Vietnam remained the longest running story of 1972. In October, following years of intransigence, North Vietnam for the first time began serious negotiations with the United States toward an agreement to end the war.

The mining of enemy harbors, the crushing of an invasion of the South and stepped-up bombing of the North apparently combined to bring about a change in Hanoi's refusal to seek a negotiated settlement. Presidential advisor Henry Kissinger met with North Vietnam's Le Duc Tho in a series of bargaining sessions late in the year, but the talks broke down in December.

TONY AUTH
Courtesy Philadelphia Inquirer

"IT'S HANOI'S CONVENTION ON RULES OF WAR!"

HY ROSEN
Courtesy Albany Times-Union

DON HESSE
Courtesy St. Louis Globe-Democrat

CURTIS — MILWAUKEE SENTINEL

TOM CURTIS
Courtesy Milwaukee Sentinel

"It's a souvenir of my visit to Hanoi."

CRAIG MACINTOSH
Courtesy Dayton Journal-Herald

'Look around you, Justice Douglas. How can you call all of this unconstitutional?'

"Jane Fonda Left Something for You!"

BILL CRAWFORD
© NEA

"And Why Not?"

ROY JUSTUS
Courtesy Minneapolis Star

'Greetings, French Liberators!'

'Greetings, Nationalist Liberators!'

'Greetings, Viet Cong Liberators!'

'Greetings, American Liberators!'

'Greetings, Government Liberators!'

'Greetings, North Vietnamese Liberators!'

GREETINGS, B-52s...

PAT OLIPHANT
Denver Post
© Los Angeles Times Syndicate

Military Backbone

HUGH HAYNIE
Louisville Courier-Journal
© Los Angeles Times Syndicate

MARLETTE
THE CHARLOTTE OBSERVER

DOUG MARLETTE
Courtesy Charlotte Observer

TONY AUTH
Courtesy Philadelphia Inquirer

ED ULUSCHAK
Courtesy Edmonton (Can.) Journal

U.S. BOMBING

CUT ON THIS LINE AND REMOVE FROM PICTURE

NORTH VIETNAMESE ALL-OUT INVASION

INSTRUCTIONS FOR ONE-SIDED PROTEST

DAN DOWLING
Kansas City Star
© Publishers–Hall Syndicate

'I'm becoming a bit confused as to who the real liberators are — the Americans liberated my arm and the North liberated my leg!'

BALDY
Courtesy Atlanta Constitution

"...IT'S DOWN TO A TRICKLE THOUGH! NOT ENOUGH TO MAKE MUCH OF A CAMPAIGN ISSUE!"

JERRY DOYLE
Courtesy Philadelphia Daily News

'I didn't think I'd eat the whole thing'

'Endangered Species'

TOM DARCY
Newsday
© Los Angeles Times Syndicate

WAYNE STAYSKAL
Courtesy Chicago Today

"WELL, I'M JUST GLAD TO BE HOME FROM THAT LOUSY WAR AND WORKING!"

THE DUMMY

ED HOLLAND
Courtesy Chicago Tribune

43

SENATE DOVES

NORTH VIETNAM

FRANKLIN MORSE
Courtesy Hearst Publications

"SAMUEL! LEAVE THAT POOR MUGGER ALONE!"

NEW SYMBOL?

MINNEAPOLIS STAR
ROY JUSTUS
Courtesy Minneapolis Star

"SAY UNCLE!"

THE BOMBING

U.S.

NORTH VIETNAM

MINNEAPOLIS STAR
ROY JUSTUS
Courtesy Minneapolis Star

ANTI-RESISTANCE PROPAGANDA

AGGRESSION

FRANKLIN MORSE
Courtesy Hearst Publications

SANCTUARY

44

Tanya of Vietnam

SCOTT LONG
Courtesy Minneapolis Tribune

DUNCE

AL LIEDERMAN
Courtesy Long Island Press

STEVE MILLER
Courtesy Honolulu Star-Bulletin

BILL SANDERS
Courtesy Milwaukee Journal

'Are we running a Defense Department
or a hire-the-handicapped program?'

ELDON PLETCHER
*Courtesy New Orleans
Times-Picayune*

TOM CURTIS
Courtesy Milwaukee Sentinel

"Why, Mr. Rogers, you really do exist!"

Kissinger's Travels

Presidential advisor Henry Kissinger commuted during the year from
Washington to Paris to Asia as peace talks and rumors of an impending
settlement of the Vietnam War continued. A week before the Presidential
election, Kissinger announced that "Peace is at hand." Subsequent events,
however, proved his prediction to be premature.

RANAN LURIE
Life and New York Times
© United Feature Syndicate

DON MOORE
Courtesy WGN-TV, Chicago

"When It's Hatched, It'll Be A Dove!"

SECRET PEACE TALKS

SUSPENDED TIL DEC. 4

RALPH VINSON
Courtesy New Orleans States-Item

NO QUESTION WHO'S KISSINGER NOW

DAME PEACE RUMORS

KISSINGER'S SECRET SAIGON MEETINGS WITH THIEU

BRUCE SHANKS
Courtesy Buffalo Evening News

48

"WHERE CAN I REACH YOU TONIGHT, HENRY?"

BASSETT
Scripps-Howard Newspapers

ED VALTMAN
Courtesy Hartford Times

The Hartford Times

'But I thought the peace talks were at the lower level'

SCOTT LONG
Courtesy Minneapolis Tribune

'I'll be damned! . . . It's Henry Kissinger!'

ART BIMROSE
Courtesy Portland Oregonian

"Buck up, they could have given it to Jane Fonda."

DRAPER HILL
Courtesy Memphis
Commercial Appeal

Baldy
BALDY
Courtesy Atlanta Constitution

'Oompf . . . this was bound to happen sooner or later'

GUERNSEY LEPELLEY
Courtesy Christian Science Monitor

THE ROAD RUNNER

DICK FLOOD
Courtesy San Jose Mercury-News

FRANK SPANGLER
Courtesy Montgomery (Ala.)
Advertiser

Watchful waiting

"NOW HERE'S MY PLAN...."

GENE BASSETT
Courtesy Scripps-Howard Newspapers

51

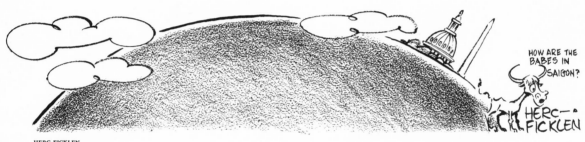

HERC FICKLEN
Courtesy Dallas Morning News

JEFF MACNELLY
Richmond News Leader
© Chicago Tribune—New York
News Syndicate

STEVE HOTCH
Courtesy San Bernardino Sun

"I'M A GOURMET COOK, TOO, DICK."

BERRY'S WORLD

© 1972 by NEA, Inc.

"You will meet a stunningly attractive girl and escort her to a party—Henry, I think I got your fortune cookie!"

JIM BERRY
© NEA

CY HUNGERFORD
Courtesy Pittsburgh Post-Gazette

JOHN SHEVCHIK
Courtesy Beaver Falls (Pa.)
News Tribune

Rough Moments With His Players

"Coo, dammit!"

DRAPER HILL
Courtesy Memphis
Commercial Appeal

54

Watergate—ITT

Police arrested five men on June 17 inside the Democratic National Committee Headquarters in the Watergate apartment complex overlooking the Potomoc River in Washington, D.C. The suspects carried cameras, two-way radios and electronic listening devices and were charged with "bugging" the offices. Three of the five men arrested had previous, although brief, connections with the Nixon Administration.

Lengthy hearings were held by the Senate Judiciary Committee early in the year over the nomination of Richard Kleindienst as Attorney General. The International Telephone and Telegraph Corporation (ITT) was alleged to have pressured the Justice Department into out-of-court settlements of several anti-trust suits against ITT. Kleindienst was accused of arranging the settlements, but no wrong-doing by Kleindienst was proved, and he was confirmed.

JEFF MACNELLY
Richmond News Leader
© Chicago Tribune—New York
News Syndicate

GENE MCCARTY
*Courtesy San Bernardino
Sun-Telegram*

Hot Line!

W. C. KING
Courtesy Chattanooga Times

'HELP! THEY KEEP ON COMING!'

CARL LARSEN
Courtesy Richmond Times-Dispatch

GUERNSEY LEPELLEY
Courtesy Christian Science Monitor

'After an exhaustive investigation I find this elephant trunk, acting independently and of its own accord, guilty of. . . .'

BILL SANDERS
Courtesy Milwaukee Journal

TOM ENGLEHARDT
Courtesy St. Louis Post-Dispatch

BERRY'S WORLD

"Oh, dear! I forgot to warn you, Harold doesn't like kidding around about the Watergate affair!"

JIM BERRY
© NEA

Open For Business

MONKEY ? WHAT MONKEY ?

ED ASHLEY
Courtesy Toledo Blade

NATURALLY, SOME THINGS SHOULD BE MADE MORE PERFECTLY CLEAR THAN OTHERS !

WATERGATE "BUGGING" INCIDENT

CAMPAIGN CONTRIBUTIONS

$25,000 FUNDS CHECK

BILL DANIELS

BILL DANIELS
Courtesy WSB-TV, Atlanta

CHARLES BISSELL
Courtesy Nashville Tennessean

DEMOCRATIC NATIO

'A Most Challenging Case, Watson!'

JACK JURDEN
Courtesy Wilmington Evening
Journal-News

GENE MCCARTY
Courtesy San Bernardino
Sun-Telegram

TATTLE TALE GREY

EDDIE GERMANO
Courtesy Brockton Daily Enterprise

'Oops, Didn't Mean to Embarrass You,
Mr. President!'

"Are You Trying to Hide Something from
the American Public?"

KARL HUBENTHAL
Courtesy Los Angeles
Herald-Examiner

ED VALTMAN
Courtesy Hartford Times

Ed Valtman 72 The Hartford Times

'But how about the girl, chief? She typed all the correspondence!'

BUD TAMBLYN
Courtesy Allentown Call-Chronicle

'Now They Want Them Put Together Again'

SCOTT LONG
Courtesy Minneapolis Tribune

'Careful not to leave fingerprints!'

Crime
and the Courts

Losses from crime and the expense of fighting it continued to soar. Thefts and burglaries cost American businesses $16 billion in 1972, and many officials voiced dire predictions for the future.

On June 29, by a 5—4 decision, the United States Supreme Court apparently banned capital punishment. The court ruled that capital punishment sentences handed out in most courts represent cruel and unusual punishment. The decision, however, was interpreted differently by the Justices voting with the majority, and the court's intention remained to be clarified.

WAYNE STAYSKAL
Courtesy Chicago Today

"WHERE'S IT ALL GOING TO END, O'BRIEN?"

MERLE CUNNINGTON
Courtesy Valley News (Calif.)

HITTING THE NAIL ON THE HEAD

ART HENRIKSON
Courtesy Des Plaines (Ill.) Herald

It's loaded!

GUNS DON'T DIE...

PEOPLE DO!

DOUG MARLETTE
Courtesy Charlotte Observer

JACOB BURCK
Courtesy Chicago Sun-Times

"THE SUPREME COURT HAS SENTENCED
YOU TO LIFE"

"IT'S BEEN RECALLED BY THE SUPREME COURT"

GENE BASSETT
Courtesy Scripps-Howard Newspapers

62

MACNELLY THE RICHMOND NEWS LEADER.

JEFF MACNELLY
Richmond News Leader
© Chicago Tribune—New York
News Syndicate

'GREAT BLOCKING IN THERE, BILL!'

PRECISION DANCING

THE NIXON
COURT
BURGER
BLACKMUN
POWELL
REHNQUIST

GENE BASSETT
Courtesy Scripps-Howard Newspapers

J. EDGAR HOOVER

JOHN RIEDELL
Courtesy Peoria Journal

SENATE CURBS ON SNUB-NOSED HANDGUNS

CRAIG MACINTOSH
Courtesy Dayton Journal-Herald

Rights
and Freedoms

Demonstrations against the Vietnam War and in support of greater individual rights and freedoms declined during 1972, but nevertheless occasionally erupted into violence. Angela Davis, tried and acquitted in connection with a courthouse shootout in California, inspired widespread protests in her behalf. Freedom of the press regained the spotlight when the Supreme Court ruled that newsmen could be required to disclose confidential news sources.

KARL HUBENTHAL
Courtesy Los Angeles
Herald-Examiner

STRANGE PHENOMENA

EUGENE CRAIG
Courtesy Columbus (O.) Dispatch

JEFF YOHN
Courtesy Sacramento Union

'Brothers' under the Skin

DICK WALLMEYER
Long Beach Press-Telegram
© Register and Tribune Syndicate

LOUIS GOODWIN
Courtesy Columbus (O.) Dispatch

'I'm Aiming at the Apple'

DON HESSE
Courtesy St. Louis Globe-Democrat

As *Hy Rosen* Sees It

HY ROSEN
Courtesy Albany Times-Union

" YOU CAN WRITE ANOTHER OBIT STORY!"

FREEDOMS SKID ROW

FOR WANT OF THE NAIL
THE SHOE WAS LOST
FOR WANT OF THE SHOE
THE HORSE WAS LOST
FOR WANT OF THE HORSE
THE RIDER WAS LOST
FOR WANT OF THE RIDER
THE BATTLE WAS LOST

AMERICAN ELECTIONS

CITIZENS FAILURE TO VOTE

R. B. RAJSKI
Courtesy Des Plaines (Ill.)
Suburban Times

SPIRO, THERE MUST BE A NON-VIOLENT WAY TO SCARE OFF THESE DEMONSTRATORS!

YOU COULD THREATEN TO FIND THEM ALL A FULL-TIME JOB!

BLAINE
Courtesy The Spectator, Canada

FREEDOM OF SPEECH

PORNOGRAPHY

JACK BENDER
Waterloo Courier
© Ben Roth Agency

"... But It's Okay Over Here?"

STOP THE BOMBING IN VIETNAM!

POLICE HEADQUARTERS

BILL McCLANAHAN
Courtesy Dallas Morning News

On Everybody's Doorstep

BILL SANDERS
Courtesy Milwaukee Journal

'Goodness! We're not trying to stifle her voice! We're just trying to purify it!'

JERRY DOYLE
Courtesy Philadelphia Daily News

BILL DANIELS
Courtesy WSB-TV, Atlanta

R. B. RAJSKI
Courtesy Des Plaines (Ill.)
Suburban Times

Wallace

Alabama Governor George C. Wallace, campaigning for the Democratic Presidential nomination, was felled by an assassin's bullets May 15 in a Laurel, Maryland, shopping center. Wounded four times, Wallace survived the shooting, but suffered paralysis of the lower body. Doctors offered little hope that he would ever walk again. He withdrew from the campaign, but addressed the Democratic National Convention in July from a wheel chair.

GIB CROCKETT
Courtesy Washington Star

SHEDDING SEASON

BOB TAYLOR
Courtesy Dallas Times Herald

DAVID SIMPSON
Courtesy Tulsa Tribune

U. S. Campaign Trail

FRANK INTERLANDI
© Los Angeles Times Syndicate

BELOW OLYMPUS   By Interlandi

Again and again, until there's nothing left!

70

**Have You Faced
The Handgun Problem Lately?**

GUERNSEY LEPELLEY
Courtesy Christian Science Monitor

BURCK ©1972, CHICAGO SUN-TIMES

JACOB BURCK
Courtesy Chicago Sun-Times

LOOK — NO BRAINS

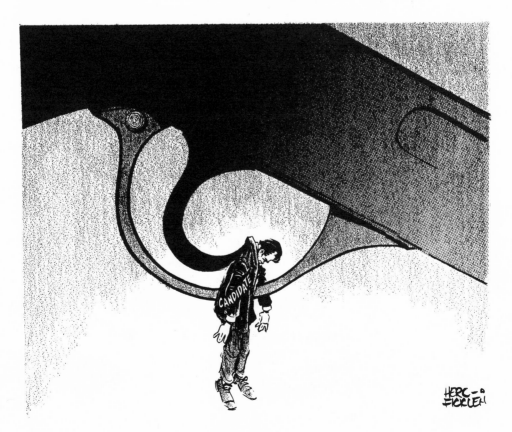

HERC FICKLEN
Courtesy Dallas Morning News

MADNESS

Another Attempt To Shoot It Out

CHARLES WERNER
Courtesy Indianapolis Star

"Go Get 'Em, Sport!"

BILL CRAWFORD
© NEA

MERLE CUNNINGTON
Courtesy Valley News (Calif.)

PUTTING ON THE BITE !

Summit Meetings

Presidential precedents were shattered in February when President Nixon journeyed to mainland China for historic talks with Chairman Mao and Premier Chou of the People's Republic of China. As a result of the meeting, relations between the two powers experienced a marked thaw.

In May, shortly after American planes had mined North Vietnamese ports, President Nixon traveled to Moscow for summit talks with the Soviets on such subjects as strategic arms limitation, trade and a joint space venture.

TOM DARCY
Newsday
© Los Angeles Times Syndicate

~AND WHEN THE TARTARS THREATENED TO CONQUER CHINA, EMPEROR SHI-HWANG-TI DECIDED~ OH, I ALMOST FORGOT, CHINA PROPER EXTENDS FROM 20° TO 40° NORTH LATITUDE AND THE LUKTCHUN BASIN IN SINKIANG IS 400 FT. BELOW SEA LEVEL AND CHARLIE CHAN'S LAST MOVIE WAS IN 1944, ANYWAY, THE EMPEROR DECIDED...'

JON KENNEDY
Courtesy Arkansas Democrat

'Look, no hands!'

ED FISCHER
Courtesy Omaha World-Herald

" . . . Is Presidential Campaign In People's Republic of China . . . "

BILL GRAHAM
Arkansas Gazette
© Ben Roth Agency

DICK FLOOD
Courtesy San Jose Mercury-News

It'll Take Practice

"WHICH ONE IS NIXON? – THOSE AMERICANS ALL LOOK ALIKE"

KARL HUBENTHAL
*Courtesy Los Angeles
Herald-Examiner*

L. D. WARREN
Cincinnati Enquirer
© McNaught Syndicate

'ON A SMOGLESS DAY YOU CAN SEE THE REVISIONARY IMPERIALIST SOVIET PIGS!'

VIETNAM
SHUFFLE,
ANYONE?

...THOUGHT
YOU'D NEVER
ASK!!

POLICY
THAW
TOWARD
CHINA

BILL
DANIELS

BILL DANIELS
Courtesy WSB-TV, Atlanta

KEN ALEXANDER
Courtesy San Francisco Examiner

"How do poker players make out against
mah-jongg players?"

"BECAUSE IT'S THERE"

The Touring Chinese Visitor

JOHN SHEVCHIK
Courtesy Beaver Falls (Pa.)
News Tribune

'Is American Fortune Cooky!'

CHARLES WERNER
Courtesy Indianapolis Star

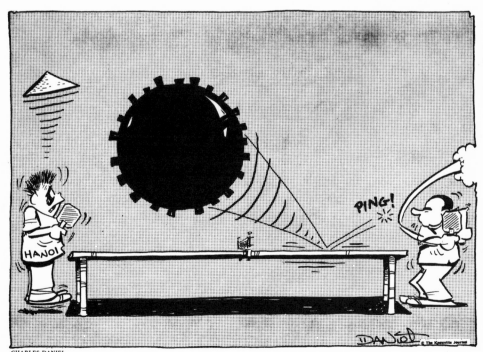

CHARLES DANIEL
Courtesy Knoxville Journal

NAN LURIE
e and New York Times
United Feature Syndicate

ED HOLLAND
Courtesy Chicago Tribune

Scorched a Little

JOHN COLLINS
Courtesy Montreal (Can.) Gazette

Moscow happiness button

JOHN COLLINS
Courtesy Montreal (Can.) Gazette

Madame butterfly

CHARLES DANIEL
Courtesy Knoxville Journal

NIXON-KOSYGIN DOCKING

BOB HOWIE
Courtesy Jackson (Miss.) Daily News

"One short step for a man but a giant stride for a presidential candidate."

ROBERT CHAMBERS
Courtesy Halifax (N.S.)
Chronicle-Herald

"Docking" experiment

REG MANNING
Courtesy Arizona Republic

PEACE OFFERING!!

BOB MURPHY
Courtesy Manchester Union-Leader

ART BIMROSE
Courtesy Portland Oregonian

"How do we follow an act like that?"

JOHN SHEVCHIK
Courtesy Beaver Falls (Pa.)
News Tribune

TOM CURTIS
Courtesy Milwaukee Sentinel

PUTTING THE FUSE OUT

"Excuse me, Miss, but I was just passing by . . ."

GENE MCCARTY
Courtesy San Bernardino
Sun-Telegram

CHINA PANDAS GO TO THE WASHINGTON ZOO

CHARLES BISSELL
Courtesy Nashville Tennessean

"HERE'S YOUR SECOND CHOPSTICK - NOW YOU CAN START YOUR FEAST"

RANAN LURIE
Life and New York Times
© United Feature Syndicate

CONVERT?

ELDON PLETCHER
*Courtesy New Orleans
Times-Picayune*

JAMES MORGAN
Courtesy Spartanburg Herald-Journal

"DIDN'T YOU KNOW COMRADE? WE'RE TIDYING-UP FOR NIXON'S VISIT!"

BOB PALMER
*Courtesy Springfield (Mo.)
Leader-Press*

'I'm Sure You Can Squeeze in Here'

JOHN STAMPONE
Courtesy Army Times

AL WETZEL
American Opinion
ⓒ Ben Roth Agency

ED ULUSCHAK
Courtesy Edmonton (Can.) Journal

JAMES MORGAN
Courtesy Spartanburg Herald-Journal

Who Says We're Up The Creek Without A Paddle?

BUD TAMBLYN
Courtesy Allentown Call-Chronicle

HAROLD MAPLES
Courtesy Fort Worth Star-Telegram

INTERESTING TO WATCH!

LONG-TERM RESULTS OF PEKING MEETING

MILT MORRIS
© Associated Press

ONE SMALL STEP FOR MANKIND...

U.S.-RUSSIAN ARMS LIMITATION AGREEMENT

CHARLES BROOKS
Courtesy Birmingham (Ala.) News

WHY NOT TAKE MOSCOW A PAIR OF BOA CONSTRICTORS?

ART POINIER
Courtesy Detroit News

SERIOUS PROBLEM OF EROSION!

TAIWAN

TOKYO-PEKING PACT

U.S.-PEKING ACCORD

NATIONALIST CHINA OUSTED FROM U.N.

MAINLAND CHINA SEATED BY U.N.

MILT MORRIS
© Associated Press

HY ROSEN
Courtesy Albany Times-Union

ALL IN THE FAMILY

BEN WICKS
© Toronto (Can.) Sun Syndicate

'Stop doing that to your eyes Dick and come to bed!'

The Economy

According to many observers, economic developments during 1972 laid the foundation for a period of vigorous growth and prosperity, but renewed inflation nevertheless remained a constant threat. The rise of consumer prices, although still continuing, slowed during 1972 from a rate of 6 percent to 3.1 percent annually. Food prices generally led the rise.

Controls announced by President Nixon in August of 1971 were credited by Government economists with having slowed the rate of inflation. Real pay, income after taxes and the effects of inflation, increased an average of 4 percent after virtually no gain the year preceding controls. Employment rose by 2.4 million under the controlled economy, one of the largest one-year increases in history.

'PAYROLL?! HELL, LADY, WE'RE DELIVERING THE CHOPPED SIRLOIN.'

JEFF MACNELLY
Richmond News Leader
© Chicago Tribune—New York
News Syndicate

LIQUORS

fine wines

THE COST OF LIVING IS UP ANOTHER BUCK A FIFTH—

10-14

BRICKMAN

Washington Star Syndicate, Inc.

BRICKMAN
© Washington Star Syndicate and King Features

BERRY'S WORLD

"Who's on a camping trip? With taxes and inflation the way they are—this is how we have to live!"

© 1972 by NEA, Inc.

JIM BERRY
© NEA

ED HOLLAND
Courtesy Chicago Tribune

SNIFF!
SNIFF!
SNIFF!

?

AFL-CIO'S SEARCH FOR THE CAUSE OF HIGH FOOD PRICES

© 1972 by The Chicago Tribune

Hot On The Trail

S-T-R-R-R-E-T-C-H-I-N-G YOUR DOLLAR!

FOOD PRICES

MORRIS

MILT MORRIS
© Associated Press

FRANK SPANGLER
Courtesy Montgomery (Ala.)
Advertiser

AL LIEDERMAN
Courtesy Long Island Press

"Oh, He's In There All Right And Under Control"

ROBERT GRAYSMITH
Courtesy San Francisco Chronicle

". . . oh, yes, and one last little item . . ."

"WE'RE STILL GOING UP—BUT SLOWER!"

CHARLES BROOKS
Courtesy Birmingham (Ala.) News

HERC FICKLEN
Courtesy Dallas Morning News

ROY CARLESS
*Courtesy Steel Labor U.S.W.A.,
Canada*

"Yes, Madam? May I Show You
Something in Steaks, Roasts..."

BILL GRAHAM
Arkansas Gazette
© Ben Roth Agency

"THE ECONOMY IS ON THE UPswing...."

BLAINE
Courtesy The Spectator, Canada

DISAPPEARING ACT THAT HASN'T QUITE MADE IT!

MILT MORRIS
Ⓒ Associated Press

KEN ALEXANDER
Courtesy San Francisco Examiner

"They only took expensive stuff ... a roast, coupla pounds of hamburger, some tomatoes ..."

91

The Kid

ROBERT ZSCHIESCHE
Courtesy Greensboro Daily News

"We'll Have You Up and Around in No Time!"

BILL CRAWFORD
© NEA

"I don't see why we couldn't just go on being good friends."

DRAPER HILL
*Courtesy Memphis
Commercial Appeal*

92

DAN DOWLING
Kansas City Star
© Publishers-Hall Syndicate

"HOW NEAR ARE WE TO FISCAL JUDGMENT DAY?"

" I'M SPEAKING FOR THE CONSUMER "

ART WOOD
*Courtesy U.S. Independent
Telephone Assn.*

BEN WICKS
© Toronto (Can.) Sun Syndicate

'I'm not surprised he looks
like that with today's
prices.'

STEVE MILLER
Courtesy Honolulu Star-Bulletin

HAROLD MAPLES
Courtesy Fort Worth Star-Telegram

CHRISTMAS TREE

GIB CROCKETT
Courtesy Washington Star

'WE ALL HAVE TO SHARE THE LOAD!'

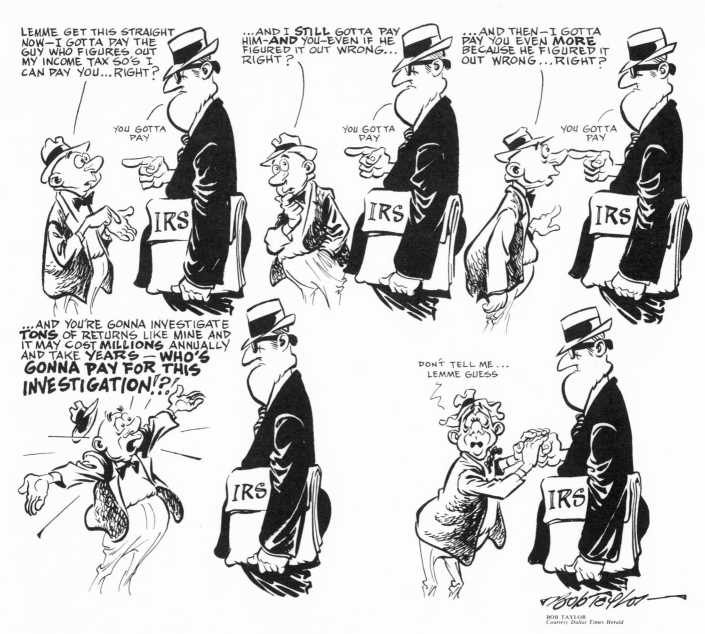

BOB TAYLOR
Courtesy Dallas Times Herald

"NOW, IT WILL TASTE MUCH BETTER!'"

ART WOOD
Courtesy U.S. Independent
Telephone Assn.

CRAIG MACINTOSH
Courtesy Dayton Journal-Herald

'WHAT'S NEXT?'

International Terrorism

Eleven Israeli athletes, in Munich to compete in the Olympic Games, were murdered September 5 by Palestinian guerrillas. The brutal act shocked the world and focused attention on the spreading problem of political terrorism. In Northern Ireland, the outlawed Irish Republican Army stepped up its attacks on British troops and civilians, and the centuries-old conflict between Catholics and Protestants threatened to escalate into full-scale war.

DAVID SIMPSON
Courtesy Tulsa Tribune

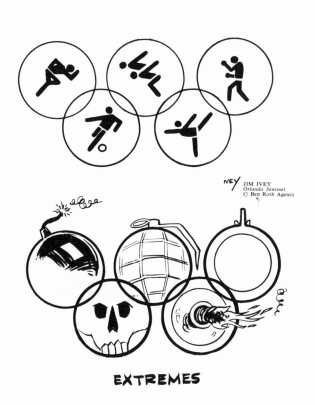

EXTREMES

JIM IVEY
Orlando Sentinel
© Ben Roth Agency

ED ASHLEY
Courtesy Toledo Blade

INTERNATIONAL BROTHERHOOD THROUGH PEACEFUL COMPETITIO

BLAINE
Courtesy The Spectator, Canada

HY ROSEN
Courtesy Albany Times-Union

IT'S ALL IN HOW YOU PLAY THE GAME

UNSCHEDULED EVENT

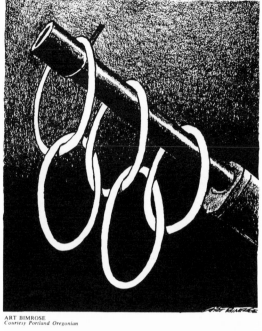

ART BIMROSE
Courtesy Portland Oregonian

DON MOORE
Courtesy WGN-TV, Chicago

© 1972 by United Feature Syndicate, Inc.

RANAN LURIE
Life and New York Times
© United Feature Syndicate

98

ART POINIER
Courtesy Detroit News

BOB PALMER
Courtesy Springfield (Mo.)
Leader-Press

BOB MURPHY
Courtesy Manchester Union-Leader

THIS POSTMAN RINGS ONCE

EUGENE CRAIG
Courtesy Columbus (O.) Dispatch

"LOOK!"

GENE BASSETT
Courtesy Scripps-Howard Newspapers

ED ULUSCHAK
Courtesy Edmonton (Can.) Journal

SHADOW OF A SCREAM

"Why didn't *we* think of using the I.R.A.?"

KEN ALEXANDER
Courtesy San Francisco Examiner

CROWN OF THORNS

BRUCE SHANKS
Courtesy Buffalo Evening News
2-8-72

"Get back where you came from Genie — you've served your purpose."

ROBERT CHAMBERS
*Courtesy Halifax (N.S.)
Chronicle-Herald*

'I'll show him. I'll cut off his end of the boat'

GUERNSEY LePELLEY
Courtesy Christian Science Monitor

JACOB BURCK
Courtesy Chicago Sun-Times

© 1972, CHICAGO SUN-TIMES

THE VICTOR

MUNICH MURDERS
URBAN SLAYINGS
ULSTER KILLINGS
VIETNAM MASSACRES

1972, CHICAGO SUN-TIMES

BLACK SEPTEMBER MORN

JACOB BURCK
Courtesy Chicago Sun-Times

"WHEN WE STOP THIS VIOLENCE WE CAN CALL OURSELVES CIVILIZED"

© 1972, Buffalo Evening News, Inc
9-13-72

BRUCE SHANKS
Courtesy Buffalo Evening News

The Drug Culture

Drug addiction continued to plague the nation in cities large and small. Estimates placed its cost to society at some $5 billion a year, with some 600,000 Americans said to be heroin addicts.

Increased efforts to legalize marijuana were made during the year, and many states softened laws dealing with its possession. Californians voted in a statewide referendum on the legalization of pot and by a two to one margin said no.

DICK WALLMEYER
Long Beach Press-Telegram
© Register and Tribune Syndicate

BURMA ROAD

ROCK-A-BYE-BABY

BEWARE OF THE PUSHER

FERRY-BOAT TO HELL

WAYNE STAYSKAL
Courtesy Chicago Today

"IMAGINE PSYCHIATRISTS SAYING POT DAMAGES THE BRAIN, ...
YOU STILL RECITE 'TREES' AS BEAUTIFULLY AS EVER!"

'The Toebone's Connected To The . . .'

ART HENRIKSON
Courtesy Des Plaines (Ill.) Herald

"I'll Drink to That!"

BILL CRAWFORD
© NEA

JACK KNOX
Courtesy Nashville Banner

Organized Labor

Unions settled for smaller pay gains in 1972 than in any other year since 1968. Many observers attributed this moderation of union demands to the President's wage-stabilization program.

Union political support, historically overwhelmingly Democratic, divided more sharply during the 1972 Presidential election campaign than it had in decades. For the first time in history, the national AFL-CIO refused to endorse a candidate, and many labor officials campaigned vigorously for President Nixon's re-election.

Professional athletes in several sports talked of organizing into unions, and major league baseball was hit by the first general player strike in history.

STEVE MILLER
Courtesy Honolulu Star-Bulletin

JEFF MACNELLY
Richmond News Leader
© Chicago Tribune—New York
News Syndicate

'GEORGE?'

CRAIG MACINTOSH
Courtesy Dayton Journal-Herald

ART POINIER
Courtesy Detroit News

IVEY
JIM IVEY
Orlando Sentinel
© Ben Roth Agency

LABOR'S LOVE LOST

JOHN RIEDELL
Courtesy Peoria Journal

Man Without a Country?

JEFF YOHN
Courtesy Sacramento Union

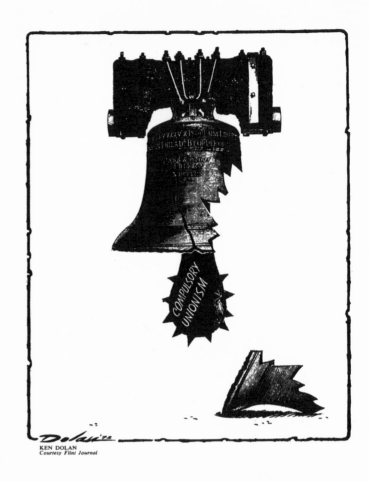

KEN DOLAN
Courtesy Flint Journal

CHARLES DANIEL
Courtesy Knoxville Journal

There Is No Joy in Mudville

W. C. KING
Courtesy Chattanooga Times

Canada

Under Prime Minister Pierre Trudeau, traditional Canadian relations with the United States and Western Europe suffered somewhat at the expense of closer bonds with the Far East. Canadian nationalism in many instances became synonymous with anti-Americanism.

"Pierre, You Come In Where It Says 'Second Fiddle.'"

DENNIS RENAULT
© McClatchey Newspapers
of California

MERLE TINGLEY
Courtesy London (Can.) Free Press

JOHN COLLINS
Courtesy Montreal (Can.) Gazette

"Which national game are we playing?"

LEONARD NORRIS
Courtesy Vancouver (Can.) Sun

"That was our machine that makes the tuning forks; and here we have our bookkeeping, accounting and legal staff handling the government inspection and license fees, excise, duty and tax records . . ."

"You're pampering yourself — get up on your feet and jog around this great
land of opportunity."

ROBERT CHAMBERS
Courtesy Halifax (N.S.)
Chronicle-Herald

LEONARD NORRIS
Courtesy Vancouver (Can.) Sun

"I know everything goes by air . . . What puzzles me is how do you get your airplanes to stay in the
air at five miles an hour?"

ROY CARLESS
*Courtesy Steel Labor U.S.W.A.,
Canada*

THE MAN FROM UNCLE

LEONARD NORRIS
Courtesy Vancouver (Can.) Sun

"He's at that awkward age ... too young for Old Age Security, too old for Opportunity for Youth grants, too late for family allowance, too conventional for Culture Council grants, too poor for tax loopholes, too rich for subsidized housing ..."

Women's Lib

The movement to gain equal rights for women achieved its greatest successes in 1972. Well-paying and responsible jobs, many of them formerly reserved for men, began to open up to women. So did most of the hazardous or so-called "muscle" jobs. Female deputies, for example, won assignments to all shifts in many sheriffs' departments. Women were employed as truck drivers and moved into construction and oil field work.

The military followed suit in August with joint announcements of widened opportunities for women in service. All Army assignments except those involving combat duty were opened to women. The Navy ended a 200-year-old tradition by assigning women to sea duty, and the Air Force admitted women into 32 of its 48 career fields.

A Constitutional Amendment banning discrimination on the basis of sex was approved by an 84—8 vote in the Senate after passing in the House the previous year.

CENE MCCARTY
Courtesy San Bernardino
Sun-Telegram

HAPPY FATHERS DAY

BOB MURPHY
Courtesy Manchester Union-Leader

'DO YOU, JOHN, PROMISE TO LOVE, HONOR AND OBEY THE EQUAL-RIGHTS AMENDMENT?'

L. D. WARREN
Cincinnati Enquirer
© McNaught Syndicate

ED VALTMAN
Courtesy Hartford Times

'But don't you see? If the Democratic Party is to stay
young and vigorous we just had to drop the abortion plank'

116

VIC RUNTZ
Courtesy Bangor Daily News

'HOLD THIS A MOMENT, SOPHIA --- I ALMOST FORGOT TO GET A MOTHER'S DAY CARD.'

WAYNE STAYSKAL
Courtesy Chicago Today

"SO WHAT IF I HAVE AN ABORTION, ADAM,... WHO'LL EVER KNOW?"

CARL LARSEN
Courtesy Richmond Times-Dispatch

"ME, sleep in that thing?... On the ground?... With all the creepy-crawlies?"

"Dirty Old Man!"

BILL CRAWFORD
© NEA

KEN ALEXANDER
Courtesy San Francisco Examiner

"Personally, I like the idea of a chick for a skipper"

MIXED REACTIONS

EUGENE CRAIG
Courtesy Columbus (O.) Dispatch

the small society   by Brickman

BRICKMAN
© Washington Star Syndicate and
King Features

Washington Star Syndicate, Inc.

118

Skyjacking

A new form of 20th century banditry, skyjacking, plagued airlines in the United States and throughout the world. Terrorists, political dissidents and common criminals attempted to commandeer more than 60 aircraft, with varying degrees of success. Before the year was over, skyjackers were demanding ransom ranging up to millions of dollars for the safe return of hijacked planes and passengers. The likelihood of an agreement between Cuba and the United States to exchange skyjackers seemed to have become a deterrent by year's end.

HUGH HAYNIE
Louisville Courier-Journal
© Los Angeles Times Syndicate

"Ah-ha! Welcome again to the lair of Wild Blue Yonder Beard!"

DON HESSE
Courtesy St. Louis Globe-Democrat

Congress should install this seat in all airliners

REG MANNING
Courtesy Arizona Republic

"Well, Sam, Do You Want To Talk To Me?"

RALPH VINSON
Courtesy New Orleans States-Item

It's Embarrassing, But It Sure Cuts Down on Hijacking

JACK JURDEN
*Courtesy Wilmington Evening
Journal-News*

Pollution

Contemporary society's three-pronged dilemma of foul air, polluted water and poisoned land continued without solution during 1972. To many, the world seemed fast becoming a spoiled globe.

The Council on Environmental Quality estimated that $287.1 billion would be required to cleanse and preserve the American environment. A figure of $5 billion was said to be the price for cleaning up the Great Lakes.

Ecological movements began to bear fruit during the year as Congress and numerous states moved toward the enactment of more stringent anti-pollution laws.

LOUIS GOODWIN
Courtesy Columbus (O.) Dispatch

LET'S PRACTICE WHAT WE PREACH

BILL McCLANAHAN
Courtesy Dallas Morning News

ROY JUSTUS
Courtesy Minneapolis Star

KEN ALEXANDER
Courtesy San Francisco Examiner

"Not So Fast, Mister!"

"It won't budge . . . we'll have to walk"

CHARLES BISSELL
Courtesy Nashville Tennessean

LEW HARSH
Courtesy Scranton Times

'. . . and when they try to stop us, people are thrown out of work'

FILTHY LUCRE

WALTER BUCHANAN
*Courtesy Columbus (O.)
Citizen Journal*

. . . and Then There's Pollution of the Mind

JACOB BURCK
Courtesy Chicago Sun-Times

DESPOILER

TOM DARCY
Newsday
© Los Angeles Times Syndicate

OH MY GOD... NOW THERE'S OIL IN THE MERCURY!

THE GRIM REAPER

GET-RICH QUICK LAND SPECULATORS

OUR DWINDLING RURAL SPACE

by GAR

GAR SCHMITT
© Gar Schmitt Syndicate

STEVE MILLER
Courtesy Honolulu Star-Bulletin

Space

Apollo 16 and 17 completed successful lunar flights, the latter of which may have marked man's last trip to the moon during the 20th century. A decision was made to direct American scientific efforts toward the development of a space shuttle system costing $5.5 billion over the next six years.

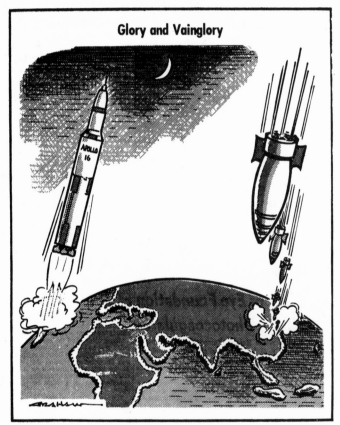

BILL GRAHAM
Arkansas Gazette
© Ben Roth Agency

ART BIMROSE
Courtesy Portland Oregonian

UNFORTUNATE COMPARISON

NO TWO-WAY COMMUNICATION ACROSS THE 79½-INCH PARIS PEACE TABLE!

PERFECT TWO-WAY COMMUNICATION ACROSS 255,617 MILES

LEW HARSH
Courtesy Scranton Times

VIC RUNTZ
Courtesy Bangor Daily News

PEACE in VIETNAM

SO MUCH HARDER GETTING LAUNCHED

Sometimes Only as High as the First Limb

MAN'S SCIENTIFIC ACHIEVEMENTS

WILLINGNESS TO KILL

HAROLD MAPLES
Courtesy Fort Worth Star-Telegram

Busing

The problems involved in busing school children found no effective solution in 1972. The House approved an Administration bill to restrict crosstown busing of students to desegregate public schools, but the measure died in the Senate.

BOB MURPHY
Courtesy Manchester Union-Leader

DEMOLITION DERBY

BALDY
Courtesy Atlanta Constitution

DOUG MARLETTE
Courtesy Charlotte Observer

"You were busted? Oh, that's a relief — for a second there I thought you said you were bused!"

Hit-And-Run Driver

TOM ENGLEHARDT
Courtesy St. Louis Post-Dispatch

HERC FICKLEN
Courtesy Dallas Morning News

DEEPER AND DEEPER

CHARLES DANIEL
Courtesy Knoxville Journal

"WILL THERE BE A BUS SOON FOR ASSIGNED NEIGHBORHOODS?"

FRANKLIN MORSE
Courtesy Hearst Publications

TOM DARCY
Newsday
© Los Angeles Times Syndicate

'The Administration says if this doesn't destroy Hanoi's unity . . . nothing will!'

JON KENNEDY
Courtesy Arkansas Democrat

Any old port in a storm

SCOTT LONG
Courtesy Minneapolis Tribune

'Where do you think you're going? . . . To a fire?'

How did your school handle busing, Grandpa?

WE WALKED.

RegMANNING

REG MANNING
Courtesy Arizona Republic

MILLAGE IS SOMETHING EVERYBODY VOTES AGAINST,
THAT A KID CAN'T GET EDUCATED WITHOUT!

ART POINIER
Courtesy Detroit News

SCHOOL CLOSED NO FUNDS

SCHOOL BUSING

KNOTTY ISSUE.. CHASE

JOHN CHASE
Courtesy WDSU-TV, New Orleans

FRANK SPANGLER
Courtesy Montgomery (Ala.)
Advertiser

ANTI-BUSING VOTE

'Your whiskers are on fire - Uncle!'

Bobby Fischer

The world focused its attention upon an unlikely spectator sport as America's Bobby Fischer wrested the world chess championship from Russia's Boris Spassky in a tempestuous 21-game series in Iceland. The temperamental 29-year-old from Brooklyn became the first American to hold the championship since the title was established in 1886.

BLAINE
Courtesy The Spectator, Canada

JIM IVEY
Orlando Sentinel
© Ben Roth Agency

'YOU'RE STILL THE CHAMP, BORIS ••• OF THE SIBERIAN CHESS LEAGUE, THAT IS'

ELDON PLETCHER
*Courtesy New Orleans
Times-Picayune*

BERRY'S WORLD

JIM BERRY
© NEA

"Dear, promise me you're not thinking of suggesting any moves to Bobby Fischer!"

ED FISCHER
Courtesy Omaha World-Herald

FRANK INTERLANDI
© Los Angeles Times Syndicate

BELOW OLYMPUS **By Interlandi**

"Boris Spassky! What are you doing here?"

'At Least We Don't Have to Worry About the Question: Will Success Spoil Bobby Fischer?'

...And Other Issues

VIC RUNTZ
Courtesy Bangor Daily News

PAP DEAN
Courtesy Shreveport Times

PAT OLIPHANT
Denver Post
© Los Angeles Times Syndicate

'OK, FILL OUT THESE FORMS AND SUBMIT YOUR PROPOSAL FOR REORGANIZING
FEDERAL BUREAUCRACY IN TRIPLICATE. WE'LL CONTACT YOU IN DUE COURSE.'

SNIPE HUNTER OF THE YEAR

BOB HOWIE
Courtesy Jackson (Miss.) Daily News

ROBERT CHAMBERS
Courtesy Halifax (N.S.)
Chronicle-Herald

GIB CROCKETT
Courtesy Washington Star

"I'm not taking any more chances!"

Requirements For A Free Nation

WALTER BUCHANAN
Courtesy Columbus (O.)
Citizen Journal

BILL SANDERS
Courtesy Milwaukee Journal

News Item: Serious crimes increase by 11% this year.

TOM DARCY
Newsday
© Los Angeles Times Syndicate

SHALL I OPEN UP ANOTHER CAN JUST TO MAKE SURE BEFORE WE BAN IT?'

TONY AUTH
Courtesy Philadelphia Inquirer

EGYPTIAN ART — 1972

BOB HOWIE
Courtesy Jackson (Miss.) Daily News

The Marx Brothers

ROBERT ZSCHIESCHE
Courtesy Greensboro Daily News

JOHN COLLINS
Courtesy Montreal (Can.) Gazette

The cairosel broke down

JACK KNOX
Courtesy Nashville Banner

CY HUNGERFORD
Courtesy Pittsburgh Post-Gazette

BILL DANIELS
Courtesy WSB-TV, Atlanta

JERRY DOYLE
Courtesy Philadelphia Daily News

PLAYING A DEADLY TUNE

'Mind If I Join You?'

DON HESSE
Courtesy St. Louis Globe-Democrat

BILL McCLANAHAN
Courtesy Dallas Morning News

ERLE TINGLEY
Courtesy London (Can.) Free Press

FRANK TYGER
Courtesy Trenton Times

"Official Washington isn't at a loss for an explanation. Being at a loss for an explanation IS official Washington policy."

DAVID SIMPSON
Courtesy Tulsa Tribune

"Wow! A Mark Spitz is one fast fish!"

MARK OF A MAN

LOU GRANT
Oakland Tribune
© Los Angeles Times Syndicate

BUD TAMBLYN
Courtesy Allentown Call-Chronicle

(Editor's note: Used on the occasion of Louis Armstrong's death)

Anything You'd Care to Mention About Old Glory's Good Qualities, Girls?

BERT WHITMAN
Courtesy Phoenix Gazette

BELOW OLYMPUS By Interlandi

FRANK INTERLANDI
© Los Angeles Times Syndicate

"Take me to America, Comrade Angela Davis — I want to be oppressed like you are!"

FOR THE BEST NONSUPPORTING ROLE

BERT WHITMAN
Courtesy Phoenix Gazette

FAREWELL CARTOON

VAUGHN SHOEMAKER
Courtesy Chicago Today

Past Award Winners

PULITZER PRIZE
EDITORIAL CARTOON

1922—Rollin Kirby, New York World
1924—J. N. Darling, New York Herald Tribune
1925—Rollin Kirby, New York World
1926—D. R. Fitzpatrick, St. Louis Post-Dispatch
1927—Nelson Harding, Brooklyn Eagle
1928—Nelson Harding, Brooklyn Eagle
1929—Rollin Kirby, New York World
1930—Charles Macauley, Brooklyn Eagle
1931—Edmund Duffy, Baltimore Sun
1932—John T. McCutcheon, Chicago Tribune
1933—H. M. Talburt, Washington Daily News
1934—Edmund Duffy, Baltimore Sun
1935—Ross A. Lewis, Milwaukee Journal
1937—C. D. Batchelor, New York Daily News
1938—Vaughn Shoemaker, Chicago Daily News
1939—Charles G. Werner, Daily Oklahoman
1940—Edmund Duffy, Baltimore Sun
1941—Jacob Burck, Chicago Times
1942—Herbert L. Block, Newspaper Enterprise Association
1943—Jay N. Darling, New York Herald Tribune
1944—Clifford K. Berryman, Washington Star
1945—Bill Mauldin, United Feature Syndicate
1946—Bruce Russell, Los Angeles Times
1947—Vaughn Shoemaker, Chicago Daily News
1948—Reuben L. (Rube) Goldberg, New York Sun
1949—Lute Pease, Newark Evening News
1950—James T. Berryman, Washington Star
1951—Reginald W. Manning, Arizona Republic
1952—Fred L. Packer, New York Mirror
1953—Edward D. Kuekes, Cleveland Plain Dealer
1954—Herbert L. Block, Washington Post
1955—Daniel R. Fitzpatrick, St. Louis Post-Dispatch
1956—Robert York, Louisville Times
1957—Tom Little, Nashville Tennessean
1958—Bruce M. Shanks, Buffalo Evening News
1959—Bill Mauldin, St. Louis Post-Dispatch
1961—Carey Orr, Chicago Tribune
1962—Edmund S. Valtman, Hartford Times
1963—Frank Miller, Des Moines Register

1964—Paul Conrad, Denver Post
1966—Don Wright, Miami News
1967—Patrick B. Oliphant, Denver Post
1968—Eugene Gray Payne, Charlotte Observer
1969—John Fischetti, Chicago Daily News
1970—Thomas F. Darcy, Newsday
1971—Paul Conrad, Los Angeles Times
1972—Jeffrey K. MacNelly, Richmond News Leader

*NOTE: Pulitzer Prize Award was not given
1923, 1936, 1960 and 1965.*

SIGMA DELTA CHI AWARDS
EDITORIAL CARTOON

1942—Jacob Burck, Chicago Times
1943—Charles Werner, Chicago Sun
1944—Henry Barrow, Associated Press
1945—Reuben L. Goldberg, New York Sun
1946—Dorman H. Smith, Newspaper Enterprise Association
1947—Bruce Russell, Los Angeles Times
1948—Herbert Block, Washington Post
1949—Herbert Block, Washington Post
1950—Bruce Russell, Los Angeles Times
1951—Herbert Block, Washington Post, and Bruce Russell, Los Angeles Times
1952—Cecil Jensen, Chicago Daily News
1953—John Fischetti, Newspaper Enterprise Association
1954—Calvin Alley, Memphis Commercial Appeal
1955—John Fischetti, Newspaper Enterprise Association
1956—Herbert Block, Washington Post
1957—Scott Long, Minneapolis Tribune
1958—Clifford H. Baldowski, Atlanta Constitution
1959—Charles G. Brooks, Birmingham News
1960—Dan Dowling, New York Herald-Tribune
1961—Frank Interlandi, Des Moines Register
1962—Paul Conrad, Denver Post
1963—William Mauldin, Chicago Sun-Times
1964—Charles Bissell, Nashville Tennessean
1965—Roy Justus, Minneapolis Star
1966—Patrick Oliphant, Denver Post
1967—Eugene Payne, Charlotte Observer
1968—Paul Conrad, Los Angeles Times
1969—William Mauldin, Chicago Sun-Times
1970—Paul Conrad, Los Angeles Times
1971—Hugh Haynie, Louisville Courier-Journal

NATIONAL HEADLINERS CLUB AWARDS
EDITORIAL CARTOON

1938—C. D. Batchelor, New York Daily News
1939—John Knott, Dallas News
1940—Herbert Block, Newspaper Enterprise Association
1941—Charles H. Sykes, Philadelphia Evening Ledger
1942—Jerry Doyle, Philadelphia Record
1943—Vaughn Shoemaker, Chicago Daily News
1944—Roy Justus, Sioux City Journal
1945—F. O. Alexander, Philadelphia Bulletin
1946—Hank Barrow, Associated Press
1947—Cy Hungerford, Pittsburgh Post-Gazette
1948—Tom Little, Nashville Tennessean
1949—Bruce Russell, Los Angeles Times
1950—Dorman Smith, Newspaper Enterprise Association
1951—C.G. Werner, Indianapolis Star
1952—John Fischetti, Newspaper Enterprise Association
1953—James T. Berryman and Gib Crockett, Washington Star
1954—Scott Long, Minneapolis Tribune
1955—Leo Thiele, Los Angeles Mirror-News
1956—John Milt Morris, Associated Press
1957—Frank Miller, Des Moines Register
1958—Burris Jenkins, Jr., New York Journal-American
1959—Karl Hubenthal, Los Angeles Examiner
1960—Don Hesse, St. Louis Globe-Democrat
1961—L. D. Warren, Cincinnati Enquirer
1962—Franklin Morse, Los Angeles Mirror
1963—Charles Bissell, Nashville Tennessean
1964—Lou Grant, Oakland Tribune
1965—Merle R. Tingley, London (Ont.) Free Press
1966—Hugh Haynie, Louisville Courier-Journal
1967—Jim Berry, Newspaper Enterprise Association
1968—Warren King, New York News
1969—Larry Barton, Toledo Blade
1970—Bill Crawford, Newspaper Enterprise Association
1971—Ray Osrin, Cleveland Plain Dealer
1972—Jacob Burck, Chicago Sun-Times